MW00718151

Iowa

Facts and Symbols

by Elaine A. Kule

Hilltop Books
an imprint of Capstone Press
Mankato, Minnesota

Hilltop Books are published by Capstone Press
151 Good Counsel Drive, P.O. Box 669, Mankato, Minnesota 56002
http://www.capstone-press.com

Printed in the United States of America.

Library of Congress Cataloging-in-Publication Data
Kule, Elaine A.
Iowa facts and symbols/by Elaine A. Kule.
p. cm.—(The states and their symbols)
Includes bibliographical references (p. 23) and index.
Summary: Presents information about the state of Iowa, its nickname, motto, and emblems.
ISBN 0-7368-0637-7
1. Emblems, State—Iowa—Juvenile literature. 2. Iowa—Miscellanea—Juvenile literature. I. Title. II. Series.
CR203.I8 K85 2001
977.7—dc21 00-020877

Editorial Credits
Erika Mikkelson, editor; Linda Clavel, production designer and illustrator; Kimberly Danger and Heidi Schoof, photo researchers

Photo Credits
Iowa Division of Tourism, 22 (top)
Jack Olson, 22 (bottom)
One Mile Up, Inc., 10, 12 (inset)
Robert McCaw, cover, 8
Root Resources/Vera Bradshaw, 12
Tom Till, 6
Ty Smedes, 14, 18
Unicorn Stock Photos/Frank Pennington, 22 (middle)
Visuals Unlimited/Glenn Oliver, 16; Dane S. Johnson, 20

Hilltop Books thanks Kathy Bowermaster at the Iowa Division of Tourism for reviewing this text.

2 3 4 5 6 06 05 04 03 02

Table of Contents

South Dakota

Minnesota

Wisconsin

Iowa River

Mississippi River

Sioux City

IOWA

Cedar Rapids

Missouri River

DeSoto National Wildlife Refuge

Herbert Hoover Presidential Library and Museum

Des Moines

Living History Farms

Des Moines River

Nebraska

Illinois

Missouri

Capital

City

Places to Visit

River

Fast Facts

Capital: Des Moines is the capital of Iowa.
Largest City: The largest city in Iowa is Des Moines. More than 194,000 people live in Des Moines.
Size: Iowa covers 56,276 square miles (145,755 square kilometers). It is the 26th largest state.
Location: Iowa is in the north central United States.
Population: 2,869,413 people live in Iowa (U.S. Census Bureau, 1999 estimate).
Statehood: On December 28, 1846, Iowa became the 29th state to join the United States.
Natural Resources: Iowa's natural resources are coal, stone, sand, gravel, and limestone. Farmers grow crops in Iowa's rich soil.
Manufactured Goods: Iowa factories make processed food, tires, and farm machinery.
Crops: Iowa farmers grow corn and soybeans. They also raise dairy cattle, beef cattle, and hogs.

State Name

Iowa's name came from a Native American tribe called the Ioway. The tribe lived mainly in the central part of Iowa along the Des Moines River valley. The Ioway lived in the area many years before European explorers arrived.

Explorers from the eastern United States traveled to Iowa in the early 1800s. In 1838, United States officials organized the Iowa Territory. This area of land was the part of Wisconsin Territory west of the Mississippi River. In 1846, the Iowa Territory became a state.

People do not agree on the meaning of the name Iowa. Some people think it means "beautiful land" in the Ioway language. Other people think Iowa could mean "here I rest."

This replica of an Ioway lodge shows how the Native American tribe lived in the 1700s.

State Nickname

Iowa's official nickname is the Hawkeye State. Some people think the name honors Chief Black Hawk, a Sauk Indian. In the 1800s, Black Hawk and his people lived in what is now Iowa. Battles with white settlers over who owned the land forced the Sauk Indians to leave in 1838. Black Hawk said, "I loved my cornfields and the home of my people. I fought for it. It is now yours. Keep it as we did. It will produce you good crops."

Other people think the nickname comes from James Fenimore Cooper's novels. Hawkeye was a character in *The Last of the Mochicans* and other books.

Iowa's other nickname comes from the state's corn crop. People often call Iowa the Tall Corn State. Iowa grows more corn than any other state. Farmers produce more than one billion bushels of corn each year. These farmers feed most of the corn crop to their livestock. They sell the rest of the corn around the world.

Iowa farmers raise corn to feed to their livestock and to sell.

THE GREAT SEAL OF THE STATE OF IOWA

WE PRIZE AND OUR RIGHTS
OUR LIBERTIES WE WILL MAINTAIN

State Seal and Motto

Iowa's government adopted its state seal in 1847. The seal represents Iowa's government. It also makes government papers official.

The seal shows a scene of the early days in Iowa. A citizen soldier stands in a wheat field. He holds an American flag in his right hand. A gun is in his left hand. The flag represents liberty. The gun means that Iowa's citizens will fight to protect their freedom. To the right of the soldier is a pile of lead and a furnace. These symbols honor the state's industries.

The Mississippi River flows in the background of the seal. An eagle flying overhead carries a banner with the state motto. Officials adopted the motto in 1847. The motto is "Our liberties we prize, and our rights we will maintain." The motto means Iowans value their freedom and will fight for it.

A plow, a sickle, and a rake appear on Iowa's state seal. These tools represent farming in Iowa.

OUR LIBERTIES WE PRIZE AND OUR RIGHTS WE WILL MAINTAIN
IOWA

State Capitol and Flag

Des Moines is the capital of Iowa. The state's capitol building is in Des Moines. Government officials meet there to make Iowa's laws.

Iowa has had three capital cities. Iowa was a U.S. territory before it became a state. The first Iowa Territory legislature met in Burlington in 1838. In 1841, the government moved to Iowa City. Lawmakers met in a building known as the Old Capitol. This building was the capitol when Iowa became a state in 1846.

In 1857, Des Moines became the state capital. The new capitol building opened in 1884. The building is made of stone from Iowa, Missouri, Ohio, Minnesota, and Illinois. A golden dome tops the capitol building.

Dixie Gebhardt of Knoxville, Iowa, designed the state flag in 1917. Officials adopted the state flag in 1921. The flag is blue, white, and red.

Iowa's flag has three vertical stripes. On the white center stripe is an eagle holding blue ribbons in its beak. The state motto appears on the ribbons.

State Bird

The eastern goldfinch is Iowa's state bird. Iowa's legislature chose the eastern goldfinch in 1933. This songbird lives in Iowa all year.

The eastern goldfinch is almost 5 inches (13 centimeters) long. It belongs to the North American goldfinch family. These birds live in the United States and southern Canada. The eastern goldfinch is the most common type of North American goldfinch.

Eastern goldfinches are colorful. In summer, the male is bright yellow. The male's head, wings, and tail are black. In winter, the male's coloring becomes darker and duller. The female has a yellow breast and an olive-brown back. The female's wings and tail are dark brown. In winter, the male and female goldfinch are almost the same color.

People sometimes call the eastern goldfinch the American goldfinch or the wild canary.

State Tree

In 1961, Iowa's government chose the oak as Iowa's state tree. The legislature selected the oak because it grows throughout the state.

Oak trees are important for wildlife in Iowa. Animals and birds find shelter in oak trees. Oak trees provide food for animals. Squirrels, deer, pheasants, and other animals eat the oak trees' acorns.

Acorns are seeds that grow on oak trees. They are rounded, smooth-shelled nuts. The acorn is pointed at one end. It is covered by a protective cap at the other end. New oak trees may grow from acorn seeds. Acorns usually do not grow on oaks until the trees are 20 years old.

Oak trees have green leaves. In the fall, the leaves change color. Most oaks can be recognized by the uneven edges of their leaves. But some kinds of oaks have smooth-edged leaves.

Oak trees grow slowly. The trees live for 200 to 300 years.

State Flower

The rose became Iowa's state flower in 1897. Iowa's government did not pick a specific kind of rose. The wild rose is considered Iowa's official flower. In 1897, Iowans gave a set of silver dishes to the battleship USS *Iowa*. Wild roses were engraved on the cups, plates, and bowls used by the officers. Iowa officials chose the wild rose as the state flower for this reason.

Wild roses grow on small shrubs throughout Iowa. The shrubs usually are 1 1/2 feet (46 centimeters) tall. Green leaves grow on the shrubs. Roses bloom on the shrubs from June through late summer. The wild rose has large pink petals. The center of the flower is yellow.

Native Americans used the wild rose for many things. They made tea from the leaves and stems. People sometimes ate the flowers. Some Native Americans used the wild rose as medicine.

Wild roses grow along roads and on prairies in Iowa.

More State Symbols

State Rock: Officials adopted the geode as the state rock in 1967. The word geode means earthlike in Latin. Geodes are round like the earth. They are 2 to 6 inches (5 to 15 centimeters) in diameter. Geodes are found in limestone. They have a hard outer shell with an inside lining of mineral crystals. Iowa has many deposits of limestone with geodes.

State Song: Iowa's state song is "The Song of Iowa." The song is sung to the tune of "Der Tannenbaum," a German folk song. S.H.M. Byers wrote "The Song of Iowa" in 1897. Iowa's state legislature adopted the song in 1911.

Southeastern Iowa is one of the state's best geode areas. Geode State Park in Henry County is named for its geode deposits.

Places to Visit

DeSoto National Wildlife Refuge

DeSoto National Wildlife Refuge is located along the Missouri River. The refuge offers shelter for migrating geese and ducks. Films and bird-viewing areas are available to visitors. Visitors hike on four nature trails.

Herbert Hoover Presidential Library and Museum

The Herbert Hoover Presidential Library and Museum is located in West Branch. Visitors may take guided tours of the library and exhibits. Visitors also view the two-room cottage where Herbert Hoover was born in 1874. He was the 31st president of the United States.

Living History Farms

The Living History Farms are located west of Des Moines in Urbandale. This large outdoor museum shows how farming in Iowa has changed during the past 300 years. An Ioway village shows how Native Americans lived in the early 1700s.

Words to Know

legislature (LEJ-iss-lay-chur)—a group of people who can make or change the laws of a state or country
migrate (MYE-grate)—to move from one place to another when seasons change or when food is hard to find
mineral (MIN-ur-uhl)—a substance found in nature that is not an animal or a plant
pioneer (pye-o-NEER)—a person who is among the first to settle a new land
prairie (PRAIR-ee)—an area of flat, grassy land with few trees
refuge (REF-yooj)—a place that gives shelter and protection
territory (TER-uh-tor-ee)—land that belongs to or is governed by another state or government

Read More

Kummer, Patricia K. *Iowa.* One Nation. Mankato, Minn.: Capstone Books, 1999.
La Doux, Rita C. *Iowa.* Hello U.S.A. Minneapolis: Lerner, 1997.
Morrice, Polly. *Iowa.* Celebrate the States. New York: Benchmark Books, 1998.

Useful Addresses

Iowa Department of Economic Development Division of Tourism
200 East Grand Avenue
Des Moines, IA 50309

State Historical Society of Iowa
State Historical Building
600 East Locust
Des Moines, IA 50319

Internet Sites

Iowa Tourism—Iowa Facts
http://www.traveliowa.com/iowa_facts

Stately Knowledge: Iowa
http://ipl.org/youth/stateknow/ia1.html

Index